RISING STARS

SCHOLASTIC INC.

New York   Toronto   London   Auckland
Sydney   Mexico City   New Delhi   Hong Kong

ISBN-13: 978-0-545-13127-8
ISBN-10: 0-545-13127-8

Published by Scholastic Inc.
SCHOLASTIC and associated logos are trademarks and/or registered trademarks of Scholastic Inc.

12 11 10 9 8 7 6 5 4 3 2 1   9 10 11 12 13 14/0

Designed by Cheung Tai
Printed in the U.S.A.
First printing, July 2009

RISING STARS

MATT RYAN

QUARTERBACK
ATLANTA FALCONS

When the Atlanta Falcons drafted Matt Ryan with the third overall pick of the 2008 NFL Draft, they were hoping he could eventually lead them back to winning seasons and eventually the playoffs. The young quarterback rewarded the Falcons with an unforgettable season that resulted in Ryan being named the Associated Press Offensive Rookie of the Year.

After losing quarterback Michael Vick before the 2007 season, the Falcons fell to a 4-12 record and finished in last place in the NFC South division. The team's rebuilding plan included hiring a new head coach and drafting a fresh quarterback. The Falcons chose Mike Smith to coach the team and Ryan to be their franchise quarterback.

Ryan first caught the NFL's eye as a record-setting quarterback at Boston College. At 6-foot-4, 220 pounds, Ryan was the perfect size for an NFL quarterback, and he boasted the college statistics to back him up. Ryan passed for more than 4,500 yards in 2007, earning ACC Player of the Year honors. His 31 touchdown passes in his senior season broke the Boston College record of 27 touchdowns held by another famous quarterback, Doug Flutie.

On draft day, he took the stage in New York City as the first quarterback selected, a long way from his youth football days spent playing for teams like the Downingtown Youth Whippets, Marsh Creek Eagles, and Philadelphia Little Quakers.

After watching Ryan work in the offseason and training camp, Smith believed that Ryan could handle the pressure, naming him the first rookie quarterback to start a season since 1975.

Ryan's rookie debut could not have been better. His first NFL pass went for a 62-yard touchdown to Michael Jenkins against Detroit. The Falcons won their season opener, and Ryan was the talk of the league.

Ryan's impact continued throughout the rest of the season as the Falcons rose from the basement to become one of the NFL's best teams. While most rookie quarterbacks are not given too many responsibilities, Ryan's maturity earned him the trust of the Falcons' coaches. He soon began calling his own plays and directing the team's no-huddle offense in pressure situations.

In just his sixth NFL start, the rookie led the Falcons to a come-from-behind victory over Chicago in the final 11 seconds. Ryan completed 22 of 30 passes for 301 yards against a tough Chicago defense, but saved his best for last. With the Falcons trailing with just 11 seconds remaining, Ryan threw a perfect 26-yard pass to receiver Michael Jenkins to set up the game-winning field goal.

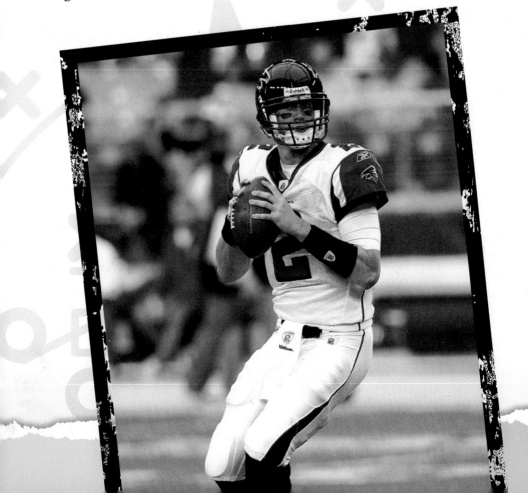

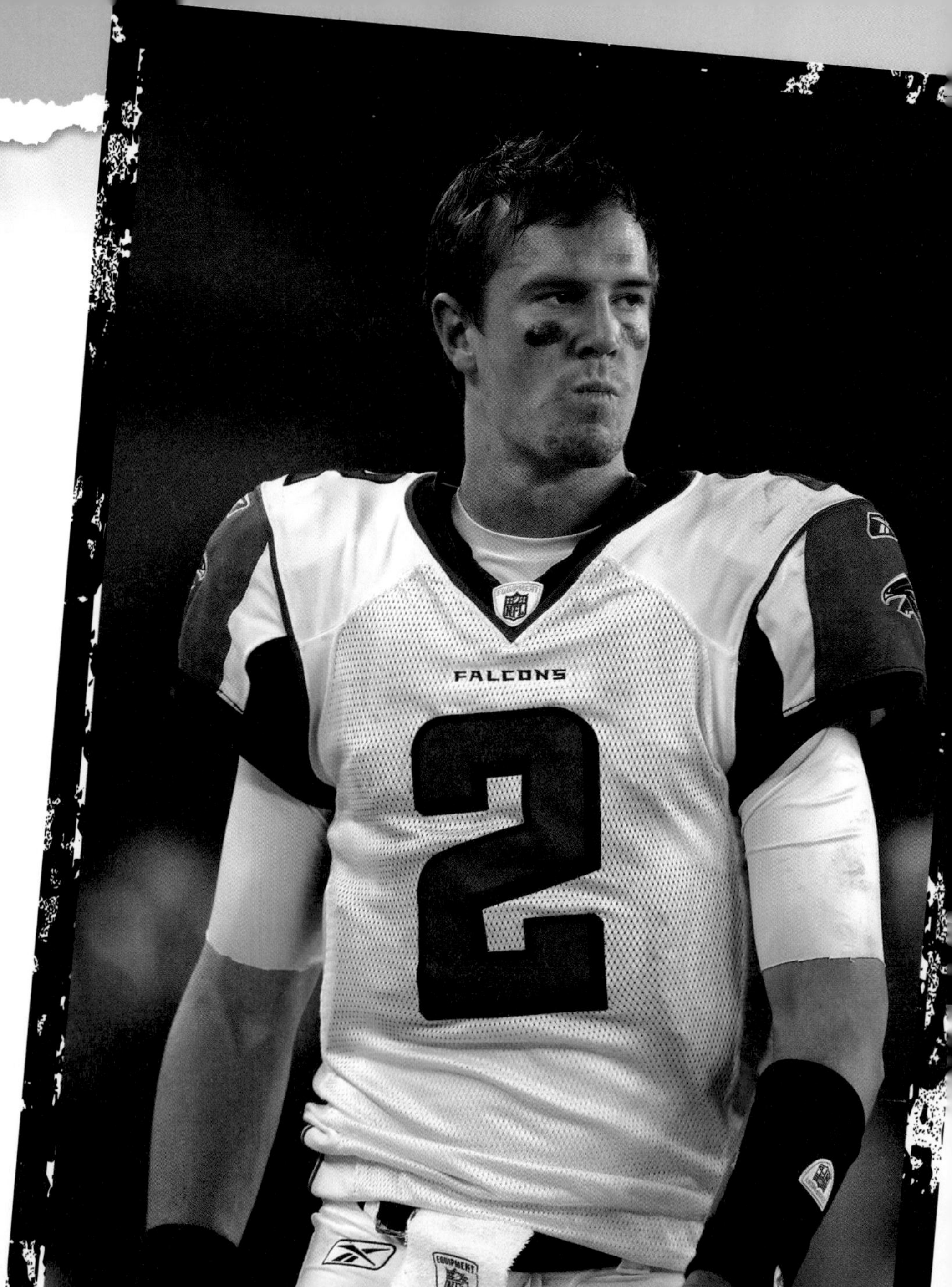
FALCONS
2

The clutch comeback gave Ryan even more confidence and the Falcons momentum. Atlanta competed for the South title most of the season before finishing 11-5 and earning a wild-card playoff berth.

Historically, the Falcons' ability to win with Ryan as quarterback was rare. Since 1960, only Pittsburgh's Ben Roethlisberger had won more games as a rookie starting quarterback than Ryan. Ryan and the Baltimore Ravens' Joe Flacco joined Rick Mirer, Peyton Manning, and David Carr as the only rookie quarterbacks to start 16 games.

Atlanta's improvement was keyed by a running attack led by free agent Michael Turner and Ryan's pinpoint passing. Ryan's final statistics were remarkable for a rookie. He ranked 11th in passer rating at 87.7 and had 16 touchdowns to go with 11 interceptions. But more important than his statistics are his grasp of the offense, command of the huddle, and veteran-like leadership.

Ryan apparently learned to be a leader in high school. While playing as a three-year starter for William Penn Charter School in Philadelphia, he was not only captain of the football team, but also the baseball and basketball teams as well.

His leadership qualities were never more evident when Ryan accepted the Rookie of the Year award.

"I'm certainly flattered," Ryan said. "There's a number of guys who had great rookie seasons this year, so to even be mentioned in that light is nice. It's certainly a great honor, and I think it speaks to what we did as a team this year."

JOE FLACCO

oe Flacco had a lot to prove during his rookie NFL season. The little-known quarterback came to the league from the University of Delaware, where he was the school's second all-time leading passer, throwing 41 touchdown passes and just 15 interceptions while leading the Blue Hens to the Division I-AA championship game. Although Flacco's statistics were impressive, many fans and scouts wondered if a quarterback from a smaller Division I-AA school could make it in the NFL.

Flacco began to answer those questions at the Senior Bowl, where NFL scouts watch the nation's best college players practice and play before the NFL Draft. Flacco passed and played well enough to shoot up the draft charts, where the Baltimore Ravens selected him with the 18th pick.

At 6-foot-6, Flacco stood out as the biggest quarterback in the draft. He could see and throw above onrushing defensive linemen and survive the pounding passers often take in the pocket. The Ravens also were impressed with his accuracy and ability to throw the long ball with the touch of a finesse passer.

Even though Flacco started training camp as the Ravens third-string quarterback, he soon found himself in the spotlight when a string of injuries forced him to start a preseason game. While he played well enough to be the Ravens' starting quarterback when the regular season began, Flacco's future as an NFL quarterback was still unclear.

Early on, Flacco's initiation to the NFL game wasn't easy. He suffered growing pains at first, throwing seven interceptions and one touchdown in his first five games. But Flacco didn't give up. He kept working hard in practice and, in his seventh game, enjoyed a breakthrough, passing for 232 yards and a touchdown in a win over the Miami Dolphins. One statistic was most important: Flacco helped lead the Ravens to wins in six of his first nine NFL games.

The Ravens offense took flight when head coach John Harbaugh took a chance on giving Flacco more responsibilities on the field. He saw that during both good times and bad times, Flacco played with confidence and composure. Even though Harbaugh was a rookie head coach, he gave his young quarterback the freedoms usually reserved for veterans.

His trust paid off when Flacco helped the Ravens win nine of their last 11 regular-season games including a 27-7 victory over the Jacksonville Jaguars in which he completed 17 of 23 passes for 297. With the win, Flacco and the Ravens earned a playoff berth as a wild-card team. Along the way, Flacco threw at least one touchdown pass in eight straight games, to tie Joe Namath and Babe Parilli for the third-longest rookie streak in NFL history!

In his first NFL playoff game, Flacco managed the Ravens' offense to a 27-9 victory and became the first rookie since the 1970 AFL-NFL merger to win a road playoff game.

In the divisional playoff round, Flacco doubled his postseason win total, helping the Ravens beat the Tennessee Titans, 13-10. With the game on the line, Flacco performed well in the clutch. His third-down pass to tight end Todd Heap gained 23 yards and put the Ravens in position for Matt Stover's game-winning field goal with 57 seconds remaining.

Flacco's season ended one game short of the Super Bowl when the Ravens lost to the Pittsburgh Steelers, but Baltimore fans were very optimistic about the team's future under their new quarterback.

For his outstanding efforts, Flacco was named NFL Rookie of the Year.

After proving the experts wrong and standing tall as a small-school quarterback who made it as a pro, there's no wonder why Ravens teammates and fans gave him the nickname Joe Cool.

CHRIS JOHNSON

When the Tennessee Titans entered the 2008 NFL Draft, most fans believed the team would select a receiver. When the Titans instead used the 24th pick to take running back Chris Johnson, many shook their heads in disbelief. Several NFL draft experts wondered if Johnson could be anything more than a role player as a professional. It didn't talk long for Johnson to prove the doubters and critics wrong.

As a 5-foot-11, 200-pound running back out of East Carolina University, Johnson was considered a speed back. He lived up to that label at the NFL Rookie Combine, where he dazzled pro scouts with a time of 4.24 in the 40-yard dash. Scouts believed Johnson's time to be the fastest electronically timed 40-yard dash in the event's history.

While scouts were sold on his speed, they still wondered if he could take the punishment that defenders give out on running plays between the offensive tackles. He made believers out of the Titans when he posted a 43.5-inch vertical jump and a 375-pound bench press. The Titans were convinced that Johnson could be an every-down running back, and he soon proved them right.

Johnson's quickness through the hole and ability to break away for long runs caused coaches to compare him to Hall of Fame running back Tony Dorsett, who rushed for 12,739 yards mainly with the Dallas Cowboys. But Johnson also gave Titans quarterback Kerry Collins a passing option out of the backfield, showing the soft hands of a receiver and drawing comparisons to versatile running backs like Philadelphia's Brian Westbrook.

Johnson learned the art of catching passes after a turf toe injury forced him to play receiver his junior season at East Carolina. He switched back to running back as a senior where his 227.7 all-purpose yards per game led the NCAA and set a Conference USA record.

Johnson quickly showed he could be a versatile NFL playmaker, racing 66 yards for a touchdown in his first professional preseason game. In his regular-season debut, he scored his first NFL touchdown on a 20-yard catch-and-run against the Jacksonville Jaguars. He proved he could carry the Titans' running game, recording his first NFL 100-yard rushing game in Week 2 against the Cincinnati Bengals, but that was just the beginning. There was more to come. Johnson turned in his best game of the season in Week 6, rushing for 168 yards on just 18 attempts, including another 66-yard touchdown gallop, against the Kansas City Chiefs.

Johnson complemented the power running of LenDale White, earning them the nicknames Smash 'n' Dash, and gave the Titans one of the most talented backfield combinations in the NFL.

Johnson earned national exposure on Thanksgiving Day when

he broke away untouched on a 58-yard touchdown against the Detroit Lions. In all, he reeled off four runs of more than 30 yards and three of more than 50 yards.

Most important, the addition of Johnson's break away ability boosted the Titans' offense, which, along with one of the league's best defenses, helped the team jump out to a league-best 10-0 record to start the season.

That amazing start helped Johnson and the Titans win the AFC South division title and advance to the playoffs. Johnson made an impact in the divisional playoff game against the tough Ravens defense, ripping off a 32-yard run and the team's only touchdown.

After an injury forced Johnson to the sidelines, the Ravens slowed the Titans offense enough to end their season with a last-minute field goal.

Johnson finished his first rookie regular season eighth among NFL rushers with 1,228 yards, averaging 4.9 yards per carry, the league's best among players with at least 250 attempts.

He became the third running back in the Houston/Tennessee franchise's history to rush for 1,000 yards as a rookie, following Earl Campbell (1,450 yards in 1978) and Eddie George (1,368 yards in 1996).

Johnson's dream rookie season also included an all-star nod when he became just the second rookie — again joining Campbell — in franchise history to be voted to the Pro Bowl.

MATT

Matt Forté enjoyed an NFL debut most rookies can only dream of. On his fourth carry as a pro, the 6-foot-2, 216-pound running back slashed through the Indianapolis Colts defense, and rumbled and raced 50 yards for a touchdown. Better yet, Forté helped the Bears beat the favored Colts, 29-13.

It was an unforgettable beginning for Forté, who went on to gain 1,238 rushing yards and 477 receiving yards, breaking the Bears' rookie combined yards record set by Hall of Famer Gale Sayers.

Forté made more history in becoming just the seventh running back in NFL history to rush for more than 1,000 yards and catch more than 50 receptions in the same season.

The Bears were merely looking for a running back to compete for playing time when they drafted Forté in the second round with the 44th overall pick. The Bears were impressed with his career at Tulane University and the fact that he stayed in school to play all four years.

FORTÉ

There was no secret as to why Forté did not leave college early for the NFL. He enjoyed playing at the same college where his father, Gene, played from 1975-77. Having led the Green Wave in rushing yards and carries his first three years, he wanted to prove that he was worthy of a high NFL Draft pick. Forté succeeded as a senior, rushing for 2,127 yards, the seventh best season in NCAA history.

When Forté joined the Bears for training camp, he was number three on the running backs depth chart. By the time the season started, he was the Bears starter. He impressed Chicago coaches with his knowledge of the offense, including blocking schemes, his toughness, and his ability to hold on to the ball when the Bears' tough defenders tried to pry it out of his hands during practice.

After his impressive start against the Indianapolis Colts, Forté and the Bears' offense struggled a bit, losing three of their next five games. The Bears struggled to pass the ball, so defenses keyed on Forté, who fought through tacklers while being held to less than 100 yards in each of the next six games.

After the Bears rested during their bye week, Forté ripped off 126 yards, contributing to Chicago's victory over the Detroit Lions. It began a streak of six games in which he regained his step, averaging 4.6 yards per carry. After Forté gained 132 yards on just 20 attempts in a win against the St. Louis Rams, the Bears found themselves in the race for a playoff berth that included a showdown with the Green Bay Packers at Soldier Field.

In the next-to-last game of the 2008 season, Forté found the going tough, gaining just 20 yards through three quarters, and the Bears trailed their NFC North rivals with the season hanging by a thread. Forté and the Bears offensive line took over. The rookie running back rushed for 52 yards in the fourth quarter, carrying the ball on seven of eight plays, and even converted a fourth-and-1 run to keep the Bears' drive and hopes alive. Forté brought the Bears crowd to its feet when he scored the game-tying touchdown with just 3:11 remaining.

But Forté's big night wasn't over. In overtime, he helped the Bears complete their comeback on the ground and through the air. Forté set up the Packers' defense with the run before catching a 14-yard swing pass that set up Robbie Gould's 38-yard game-winning field goal.

The importance Forté played in the Bears' offensive attack was as clear during this must-win game. Forte gained 101 of the Bears' 210 total yards of offense against the Packers.

After Chicago's season ended in a disappointing loss to the Houston Texans, Forté's contributions were amazing for a rookie.

Throughout the season, he touched the ball in 51 percent of the Bears' runs or throws — the highest percentage among all NFL running backs.

Having graduated as an NFL rookie running back, Forté took time out to secure his off-the-field future by returning to Tulane University to continue working toward a finance degree and college diploma.

JEROD MAYO

LINEBACKER
NEW ENGLAND PATRIOTS

Most NFL teams have adopted a defensive system that uses a linebacker's best skills in special situations. Some linebackers specialize as run-stoppers who play first and second downs. Others are speed rushers who enter the game on third-down passing situations. It's become rare for linebackers to play every down, but don't tell that to Jerod Mayo. As a rookie, Mayo became an every-down linebacker for the New England Patriots.

Mayo's versatility at inside linebacker isn't surprising to the Patriots, who selected the 6-foot-1, 242-pounder with the 10th overall selection in the 2008 NFL Draft. After watching Mayo stuff college offenses while playing middle linebacker for the University of Tennessee, the Patriots knew he could fit into their 3-4 defensive alignment.

His early success also wasn't a surprise to Mayo, who told reporters that he was a "really confident" player who expected to contribute right away, after he was drafted.

Mayo also admitted that he wanted to be named Defensive Rookie of the Year, a bold claim for any rookie defender considering that no Patriot had won the award since Hall of Fame cornerback Mike Haynes in 1976.

Mayo, who was an All-American linebacker and running back at Kecoughtan High School in Hampton, Virginia, first attracted the attention of NFL scouts at Tennessee where he was the Volunteers' best defender. After earning All-American and All-Southeastern Conference honors, many teams moved Mayo high on their draft charts, but some experts were still surprised to see the Patriots draft him so high in the first round.

Mayo quickly impressed Patriots coach Bill Belichick with his maturity and preparation during training camp. After playing well in preseason games, Mayo was made a rookie starter by Belichick and his staff. He was surprised to be playing next to veteran Patriots linebackers Tedy Bruschi and Mike Vrabel, who had starred in three New England Super Bowl victories.

It didn't take long for the rookie Mayo to become perhaps the Patriots' best linebacker when he played every down of his second NFL game. While other Patriots linebackers rotated on and off the field depending on the down and situation, Mayo had proved to the Patriots that he could play well against the run and the pass.

Mayo's work ethic off the field is one reason why he excelled as a rookie. He quickly gained a reputation for spending many hours studying videotapes of games and his defensive assignments. By being prepared mentally, Mayo is able to better recognize an offense's habits and take advantage of his quickness and speed in getting to the ball carrier or passer.

"Jerod has been a pleasure to coach," Belichick said. "From the day he arrived, Jerod has been mature and extremely dedicated to his profession, and those qualities translated into consistent production on the field."

Mayo ended up starting all 16 games in his rookie season and even led the Patriots in tackles with 139. His performance only improved as the season unfolded. In December, he led the Patriots with 35 tackles and helped the team win four straight games. In the final game of his rookie season, he made an amazing 23 tackles — 17 solo — against the New York Jets. It was the most tackles by a Patriot since 1994. He finished the season ranked as the NFL's leaders in tackles and gave Patriots fans reason to believe that they will be watching yet another great linebacker for many seasons to come.

While Mayo was disappointed that the Patriots did not reach the playoffs, he did manage to fulfill a preseason dream and prediction when the Associated Press named him Defensive Rookie of the Year.

CHRIS HORTON

SAFETY
WASHINGTON REDSKINS

Chris Horton had to wait a long time to hear his name called at the 2008 NFL Draft, but he didn't take long to make a name for himself as a rookie.

Horton watched as 248 other players were drafted before the Washington Redskins used their seventh-round — and last draft pick — to select him. He felt lucky to be given the chance to play professional football and made the best of his opportunity.

Horton first proved his talents as an All-American safety at UCLA where he gained the reputation for being one of the Pac-10's biggest hitters. At 6-foot-1, 211 pounds, Horton hit more like a linebacker when plugging the holes on running plays, but possessed enough speed and quickness to cover receivers going deep. He was also known for knocking receivers out of games with hard hits. But it was a pre-draft meeting that really impressed Redskins coaches. They believed his excellent work habits and sharp football mind could make him a valuable backup safety and strong special teams contributor. As it turned out, the Redskins got much more in Horton.

In the Redskins Hall of Fame preseason game, Horton made the best of his first chance to show off his football smarts on his first NFL play. He correctly guessed that the Indianapolis Colts would attempt an on-side kick and recovered the ball after several teammates missed. He also made Redskins coaches take notice of his potential when he contributed a pair of quarterback sacks on safety blitzes and four tackles.

The performance helped Horton secure a place on the Redskins regular-season roster as a backup safety and special teams player, but the rookie wanted more. He knew that he needed something else to compete for a starting spot.

Before the regular season started, Horton called his former UCLA defensive coordinator DeWayne Walker and asked for advice. He hoped that his old coach — who was also a former Redskins assistant for head coach Joe Gibbs — could give him some tips on how he could be a good pro. Because the Redskins were using the same defensive system as the Bruins, Walker knew that all Horton really needed was to trust his instincts.

That advice proved valuable in Week 2 when the Redskins needed him to replace a sick starter. Playing against the New Orleans Saints — the team Horton had grown up watching — the rookie turned in a memorable debut. The rookie picked off two interceptions, recovered a fumble, and made a crucial third-down tackle in the Redskins' 29-24 win over the Saints. The performance earned him the NFC's Defensive Player of the Week award.

When Horton topped those accomplishments with a fourth-quarter interception of quarterback Tony Romo that led to the game-winning field goal and 26-24 upset victory over the NFC East rival Dallas Cowboys, Redskins fans hailed a new hard-hitting hero.

Redskins players and fans soon gave Horton a nickname — Predator — in honor of his dreadlocks hairstyle and sense for hunting down ball carriers and receivers. The rookie selected with the fourth-to-last pick was also earning fans across the NFL. His four takeaways in his first two professional starts also earned him recognition as the NFL Defensive Rookie of the Month.

Horton never gave up his starting positions, roaming the Redskins secondary, striking fear into the hearts of receivers and running backs. He also developed a knack for making big plays such as his three interceptions, third most among NFL rookies.

The Redskins did not make the playoffs, but Horton earned post-season honors, including being named to several All-Rookie teams.

Part of Horton's motivation to succeed as a professional football player is based on his experiences growing up in New Orleans. He played football and ran track at De La Salle High School, where he was the Most Valuable Player after leading the team in tackles, forcing 12 fumbles and even blocking seven kicks in 10 games during his senior season.

In 2005, Hurricane Katrina struck the New Orleans area. Most of Horton's family evacuated to Texas, but his great-grandfather remained to ride out the storm. The hurricane's heavy winds knocked a tree through the roof of Horton's family's home. Most of the family's possessions were destroyed and his great-grandfather was killed. Horton's family returned to Louisiana and he continues to honor his late great-grandfather today.